# The Freedom in
# DRAGONFLIES

# The Freedom in
# DRAGONFLIES

# Bridgette L. Huitt

Trilogy Christian Publishers

A Wholly Owned Subsidiary of Trinity Broadcasting Network

2442 Michelle Drive

Tustin, CA 92780

For information, address Trilogy Christian Publishing

Rights Department, 2442 Michelle Drive, Tustin, CA 92780.

For information about special discounts for bulk purchases, please contact Trilogy Christian Publishing.

Trilogy Disclaimer: The views and content expressed in this book are those of the author and may not necessarily reflect the views and doctrine of Trilogy Christian Publishing or the Trinity Broadcasting Network.

10 9 8 7 6 5 4 3 2 1

Library of Congress Cataloging-in-Publication Data is available.

ISBN 979-8-89333-968-0

ISBN 979-8-89333-969-7 (ebook)

# DEDICATION

To all of those in my life who have encouraged me to fulfill my God-designed purpose even when things were dark. Thank you....

To my daughter: May you always seek God and know that He is with you in every breath you take....

### AND

A special thanks to RPMx Construction for your generous donation to help show the love of God through my story!

# TABLE OF CONTENTS

# INTRODUCTION

To the unknowing eye, I organize my affairs well. However, if I told you every challenge, every thought, and every feeling I have during the day, you would see I am just like you in most aspects. In fact, as I am writing about my journey of abuse and healing, I am presently trying to navigate more things life has thrown at me. We will all do this for the rest of our lives if we are truly seeking growth. Growth is uncomfortable. We should embrace the blessings of life, even if we are not currently in a season of rest. If you are looking for a book that is going to tell you how to feel perfect every day, *go back to the bookstore*. This is not it. This book is about every experience that shaped me and how I could have been shaped so much differently if it were not for Christ. This is my rescue story and about how even amid the current storm, I can choose a joyful, peaceful life, because greater is He that lives in me than he that is in the world (1 John 4:4). My life is a testament to that Scripture.

The world can offer so many shiny things! I will be 100 percent honest and say I lived an "exciting" life when I was in and of the world; there were also extremely scary times I realized I should have died. When I was living that life, there was chaos present daily. I was working hard, playing harder, and never stopping to consider much beyond the current moment or feeling. I had big plans for how my life would go, but I veered off the path intended to give me the most abundant life. Various decisions made by me and by others with "free will" caused me to venture down paths that weren't on my map. The results had me asking more than once, "What if I had not chosen that? Where would that decision have led?" Do yourself a favor and do not go down the path of "what if." It is a closed road the moment you make your choice. Living in regret is a burden we cannot carry without negative side effects and serves no purpose other than stopping us from fulfilling our God-given purpose. Learning from our past mistakes and making the effort to not repeat them is the way to continued growth.

# CHAPTER ONE

From the moment I was in the woman's womb who holds the title "mother" for me, the world would say that I was doomed to a bad life. Born into a volatile atmosphere, I could not protect myself. Thank God for my seven-year-old brother, but what he had to endure to protect us breaks my heart, even forty-six years later. It was my brother who saved me. He is my half-brother by blood, but he never acted like half of anything. He was just a little boy, in the thick of it, trying to protect his sisters. Alcoholic, abusive parents brought me home. I remember my mother trying to protect us as much as she could, but she could not even protect herself. Because of frequent and brutal beatings, my mother had dentures at twenty-eight after my father kicked her teeth out with steel-toed work boots. There were no domestic violence laws then and would not be for another seventeen years. She told me about one time she took a stand against him—I believe before I was born but after the birth of both of my sisters. He had just beaten her for the third time that week the night before. When he, drunk and ready to heap another round of abuse on her and my siblings, came into the house, she was at a new break-ing point that day and was determined that would be the day *she* ended the abuse. She drank vodka for a while before he was due home—liquid courage. I cannot imagine the depth of fear inside her. She told me she had a large lead-crystal lamp by the bed and grabbed it when she heard him ascending the stairs. As soon as he came around the corner into the room, she swung the lamp and hit him on the head, knocking him down. She waited a few minutes to see if he was coming after her, but he remained still, on the floor, and blood was now coming from the wound on the side of his head. She walked over and kicked him with her foot to roll him over, and he still did not move. "That's good," she said, thinking to herself how nice it would be if he just never got up. She rolled him over again and he tumbled down the first flight of stairs and his head hit the wall of the landing. Again, when he did not move, she was hopeful. She did the same to roll him down the second flight of stairs and he hit his head a third time. Since there were not domestic violence laws to protect her or us, she called a police officer friend of hers to come over because she did not know what to do at this point. He was at the house with her in a matter of minutes to assess the situation and see if my father was dead. When he realized he was still alive and knowing the history of abuse, he sat with her and had coffee for a couple of hours. It was the only act of kindness he could offer her then. After three hours, he was still breathing, so they called it in to get him to the hospital. She would wish many times that he had died that day.

When I was twenty-nine, I went to counseling for the first time. During those sessions, I went back through what I could remember from that period in my life and the things that came up still cause me to physically shake. This is a warning. I am going to paint graphic images at points throughout my retelling of my trauma and healing.

Sitting in the counselor's office, I can hear the secondhand ticking on the clock. She asked me something about my childhood and the memories of that house came flooding back. *That house held so much trauma.* I had forgotten about that time for twenty-five years, while trying to survive the rest of my childhood, but the rage remained. The house that my mother says I cannot remember because we moved from there when I was eighteen months old, I happen to remember every tiny detail of the interior and exterior.

I remember the big oak tree in the front yard. The front door opened into the living room, garage to the right, kitchen/backyard straight ahead, and bedrooms to the left. I can still see the brown, shaggy carpet in the living room with that ugly brown with orange-striped tweed couch; so itchy. I can see the black-and-white checkered linoleum floor in the kitchen, the empty refrigerator and cabinets, and the overgrown grass in the backyard. I can smell wet and moldy laundry in the bathroom hamper. The hallway had the bathroom on the right, my brother's room farther down on the right, the room my two sisters and I shared was on the left, with my parents at the end of the hall. Memories from that place still haunt me, though I could not remember the worst of it, only the details of the home. Through counseling for two years, I learned that was my brain's way of protecting me. The memories I have of the abuse we all suffered in that house sometimes still wake me up at night, but I am blessed to reach out to God to calm my spirit and give me His peace. I used to drink to forget, and now the more I remember, the more healed I am. That is the hardest part. Feel it to heal it.

One memory is of me sitting in my highchair and my siblings looking for anything to feed me. The only thing in the house was sugar, ketchup, and baby aspirin. I remember them putting ketchup and baby aspirin on my tray and they ate some too. Even then, God was protecting us. We all could have died or ended up with Reye's syndrome.

I remember the fighting and panicked screaming and crying as he beat her. This happened on a daily repeat cycle, until he disappeared for days on his latest bender.

One day, I was sick: throwing up. I am not sure how old I was but under eighteen months, walking and talking. I went to the end of the hall. My siblings were outside, so I opened my mother's door. Her dresser was on the left wall, the head of her bed on the far wall, and he was being intimate with my mother. Strange how I knew that, even then, but I told her I was sick, and she said nothing. She just jumped up on his command to "get that little brat out of here" and closed the door in my face. She complied to protect us both. I remember mundane things too. The tapestry above the couch (dogs playing poker). Playing outside with my siblings and the neighbors, a mean babysitter locking us in the bedroom all day every day she sat for us, our dog trying to jump the fence and dying right in front of us because he received a puncture and cut an artery. The overgrown grass in the backyard, and my mother using her cigarette to draw pictures in the dark for me and my siblings. Her expression of love? Once I was sick on the couch and I wet myself. My mother came in frantically and said he was coming home soon. She instructed my brother to flip the couch cushion because, quote, "If he finds out, he's going to kill her." The first man that was supposed to set the example for how I allowed others to treat me. My *father* molested his daughters and stepson, repeatedly. I can still remember the weight of his body as he rubbed himself up against me. I remember the black widow spider tattoo he had on his chest scared me. That is when my eight-and-a-half-year-old brother knocked him out with a two-by-four to stop him. Had my brother not been there, it would have been much worse for me. Another memory recently revived is the day my father let a friend of his lay me on the living room floor and molest me on a pink blanket. I cannot tell you how many times I have questioned why my father considered it acceptable to steal a child's innocence or why people with such tendencies may become parents. The violence that took place in that house must be at least a taste of what hell is like, and the subsequent situations, hell adjacent.

Have I questioned God? A million times over. Every time, I have been answered the same because He is unchanging. He will not interfere with our free will. He gave us free will because we must willingly choose our path and that means the ability to choose to harm or heal. We must have free will because without freedom, we could not choose to follow Him, and He does not want to control us. As any parent will understand, we want our children to love us. We do not want them to be afraid or sad but thriving and happy. We also understand that means protecting them from things by teaching them what to stay away from. We want to protect them from the harmful things around them, and we have already seen where those things can lead. It means not always giving them what they think they want. God is the same.

Discussing the memories with my brother brought about very painful but healing moments for both of us. He was older, so he remembers things more vividly than I, and I feel horrible for him. He is healing too. We both agree that we healed only by God's strength when we had none, and the acceptance of His love is the only reason my brother and I still have a heart of flesh. So many grow cold against God when terrible things happen, but the fact is, He is the only one that will never forsake you. He does not operate in the confines of our humanity or created timelines or our perceptions. He does not make dreadful things happen to people. On the contrary, the power with which I have seen Him move is awe inspiring, but because we have such a limited view, we allow our mindset to remain confined to the earthly time we have. We do not see with the eternal mindset, and if we did, we could see that everything we experience is either because we are either following Gods plan or running away from it. Being on His path is not easy. I did not care for this path until I was ready to heal and grow. Now I find so much peace, even through the hardest moments, because I know He is working things out for my good. Jeremiah 29:11 tells us He knows the plans He has for us, and they are for our good. He has shown me the good He has, many times over, but it took shifting my perspective towards gratitude to understand how much He wants for us.

We both tried different numbing methods over the years. Drugs and alcohol did not help, and on the contrary, caused delay in our healing. It numbs the pain you feel, but it does not allow you to face it and heal it. Facing what happened is the only way to really accept the things that are completely unfair and never should have happened. Do not try to make sense of it by looking at it with our limited human mindset; you cannot rationalize evil.

The Bible tells us that there will be trouble. It also tells us that He that lives in us has overcome the world. He overcame death! I am not a theologian, so I will not debate every detail and verse in the Bible with you. I do not have to defend the living Word of God. I am called to tell you of the *power* of God I have experienced in my own life. You do not know me, but I know the person I would have been now if God had not been there and if I had not given everything to Him. My prayer is that by the end of this book, you will see His power in my life and ask Him to show up in yours.

My next memory was around three years old. I was sitting on the floor at the Louisiana State Building in family services. My siblings were there with me. My mother brought us to seek help to get us out of the situation finally. Remember, there were no domestic violence laws then. I know she was doing the only thing she could, but I remember being so scared. Still, she had at this point tried to leave him many times over the years with no success. I remember one time she took us and left. I am uncertain of my age then (two?), but I remember when he found us the last time. He grabbed her by her hair and drug her to his car from another car. The headlights of his car were shining brightly in my eyes. I can see their shadows; his hand gripping her hair tightly, both of her hands trying to pull her hair away from his grip and her screaming, *"Run!"* to her four small children. That man hated us and that is how I know God's hand was in it even with my father's free will; we all should have been dead. It is not like he did not try.

I am grateful to God for keeping my heart soft enough to want to help people that have been through trauma, but it is not the easiest path. It has taken a lot out of me. I have prayed for, forgiven, and helped more people who have betrayed me than I care to count. I want to say that I have forgiven my father entirely for everything that he put us through, but as I author this book and the memories continue to flow, I cannot say that is true exactly.

I believe that I have forgiven him to where I wish nothing but salvation and an eternal life with Jesus for him. That may be forgiveness, but I believe when I can remember something and not feel instant anger and shame is when I will say I have forgiven him entirely. Maybe forgetting and forgiving are not the same thing and what I am trying to do is forget. I cannot forget completely; none of us ever really do. When I can instantly dismiss the memory as soon as it comes, that is as close as I believe you can get.

# CHAPTER TWO

I remember the day that my new foster family came to get me from my family home. They pulled up in a pickup truck; the woman took me and held me, and the man talked to my mother for a minute. I did not know these people; I had never laid eyes on them. The only thing I remember thinking was, *Where am I going?* and *Where is my brother?*

I was almost four years old at the time. I remember them putting me in the back of the truck, and back in 1981, that was okay. Such a scary time to be going somewhere, and I had no idea what would happen when I got there. It was a long drive since they lived about forty-five minutes from the city we lived in at that time. When we got to their house, I just remember being scared and that was it. My next memory is of trivial things like watching TV, and I remember I could not see very well so I would pull at the corner of my eye because it changed the view, and I could see better. They noticed I was doing this, and I remember getting glasses right after that. I remember having my *first* birthday party ever when I was five. They got me new bedding that I thought was fancy at the time. Little things like her coming home from work after I was out of school and giving me a snack before dinner. It was more food than I had ever received daily since birth. I also remember wetting the bed quite often, which we know now, is a sign of the sexual abuse that I endured, but every time I did, I still got my bottom spanked. I do not fault them because child psychology was not a field parents delved into when I was little. They did not think about the emotions of children or the traumas that can bring on various physical issues. I wish I could say the trauma stopped there and I was able to live and heal, but it did not. I know my mother had to separate us and put us in different homes because no one would take us all, and I know at the time she did not really want to because she did love us and tried to protect us in those moments.

However, her behavior is not where we are now, so let us go back to the first time I met my cousin in my new family. It was a female cousin, and I looked up to her instantly. I wanted to be just like her. She was fifteen, and I was only four when I met her. My daily and weekly life was quite normal, and we would visit my foster mother's family quite often since her mother, brother, and sister all lived in the same city. Every time we would go to my aunt's house, my cousin would take me outside and play with me, showing me various bugs and such in the tall grass. But then she would take me into her room. It started out just telling me that I was so pretty, and she loved me while playing with my hair. Then it progressed to kissing my cheek or on the lips occasionally. She groomed me for a while before she had me touch her for the first time. I felt like it was wrong even in the moment, but this is what the adults in my life had done to me all my life so far, so it was not really any different than what I had already known. Even then, as a child, I knew shame. I remember spending quite a few hours in her room weekly and no one ever even came in to check on me. She did apologize and ask my forgiveness when I was seventeen. I told her, "I forgive you" and I left it at that, but it is not something that you can ever forget, is it? My foster parents took me in when they thought they could not have children, but around the age of five or six, they began having children of their own, and when their first child was two, they contacted my mother and asked her if she wanted me back. I do remember the grandmother in that family used to call me names and belittle me every time we went to their house so that may have played in the decision to return me to my mother. At the time, I did not care because I wanted to be with my mother. There were so many times when I was with that family that I did not necessarily feel like I belonged, but I was treated better than I had previously been, so I never spoke up. For the three and a half years that I lived with them, I felt more loved than I had felt before because she was an exceedingly kind woman, and he was a truly kind man.

I did get to see my oldest sister while living with them because they tried to keep me connected with her when they found out where she was. I was overjoyed to get to spend time with her! The first time they took me to see her, I was around six and I still remember her jumping up and down and sprinting to embrace me. They were doing the best they knew how and they never knew about any of the things that happened with my cousin. I visited them as adults later in life and never mentioned it then either. I truly have forgiven her for the things that she did because she must have been abused as well at some point in that family or by a church member at the

Pentecostal church that we went to. There were some at that church that were a little too close to us children.

   You would think with the things that have happened that I would have no reason to still believe that there is a loving God. How can God exist and not intervene in the case of a child? The truth is we are all given free will for a reason. Without free will, we would be puppets, and God does not want puppets. He wants to be loved because we choose to love Him. The fact is, I should have died. I did not die at the hands of others free will, but most importantly, I did not lose my compassion and hope for this world.

# CHAPTER THREE

I returned to my mother around the age of eight, and she was already married to my stepfather. They lived in a duplex in the city where I was born. At first, everyone was so happy to be reunited but something was still missing for me. I missed my siblings, and when I asked about them, my mother said my brother was returned to his father in Maryland and my middle sister had been placed permanently with another home and they had fought to keep her. I did ask if I could still see my older sister and I was told not right away. Within the first three months, she came home as well. I must admit I didn't understand that, because the family she had been placed with was very well off and seemed to love her immensely, and I remember hearing a phone conversation with my mother and her foster mother and it did not seem like she wanted to give her back, but she didn't have a choice as my mother requested her return. I suppose now that she had her life together, she did want her children back or at least as many as she could have. My sister was not happy the day she came home. I remember being so excited to see her and she just seemed so angry. We fell into the routine of daily life. My sister and I found ourselves alone a lot because my parents did work, and they also went out a lot. At that time, that is what parents did, or at least all the parents of the friends that I had. Parents continued to live their lives and children were to stay out of it and go play. We had so many fun days outside, playing in the woods next to the houses where we lived or playing down the street with other kids, riding bikes. Kids raised each other. There was always that one neighborhood mom who had all the kids at her house all the time and selflessly and lovingly provided snacks and drinks while we messed up the house and always had laughter. I am thankful for those moms because they gave me the image of what a loving mom should be.

During the first year we were back living with my mother, my stepfather came home and said that we were moving to Maryland because he had a job offer that was more money. At that time, everything was going so well, and we were happy, so we were excited about our new adventure. They sold everything that we could not fit into our station wagon, and we set off on a hilarious but tiring three-day journey to drive there. A funny couple of moments on that journey were when my mother's favorite dog that we brought with us decided to hike her leg on my head while I was sleeping. It was not funny at the time to me, but everyone else cracked up and I can see the humor now. Then my mother had the wonderful idea to cut my bangs because they were in my eyes, and it was annoying her. She was not very gentle when she cut my bangs on top of a very windy mountain. I was relentlessly teased for the next month until they grew out. Every time she would look at me, she would laugh and honestly, I did not think much of it at the time, but I could not look at my daughter and laugh at something that I did to her and tease her about it. It just does not seem like the thing that parents should do, and I do remember it made me feel sad every time someone laughed.

When we arrived in Maryland, we first lived in a townhouse with an upstairs apartment and downstairs apartment. It was small but adorable, and we had so much fun there. My sister and I managed to have fun no matter what situation we were in. There were abuses during that time, but it was not as bad as it had been when we were little.

My brother came over one day and took me and my sister for a ride in his car. We went to visit a friend of his and hung out there for a while. I was so excited to see my big brother, my protector.

We lived in the townhouse for about a year before we moved into another house that was much larger. We were so amazed to see this huge Victorian home that we had just moved into. It was so large that it had been converted into three apartments. There was an apartment above us; we were in the middle, and there was an apartment below us in the basement. The man that lived in the apartment below us was genuinely nice, but I think he was a little odd because he liked to hang out with us children. He did nothing creepy, and I believe he might have even been a music teacher, but I cannot say that for sure. He always let us spend time there and listen to music and taught us about the music. He taught us how music heals. He was one of my favorite people at the time. There was a large park next to our house so we could go and play anytime we wanted. We finally felt like we were happy as children should be. Even with the constant yelling and screaming at us about every little thing, we were still happy because we were there with my mother and loved her no matter how she treated us, as children often do. But the happiness was not to last.

About four months into living there, my stepfather lost his wallet on the Friday he was paid before he got home. At least that is what we were told. They were fighting, though he never hit my mother. We had my brother staying with us at that point for a few weeks, until his military departure date as he had joined the Army. He again came to our rescue by taking the four ingredients that we had in the house and combining them into a meal that was not exactly delicious but kept our stomachs from growling for three days before my parents made the decision to go back to Louisiana. I still remember the taste and it was not pleasant but as he always did, he made sure we were fed. Right before we were supposed to leave, the station wagon broke down and was too expensive to repair. That did not stop us from getting on a Greyhound bus to travel the distance back home. The three-day trip down there is something that I would never like to experience again. I don't know what city it was in, but I know it had been at least a full day since we had anything to eat or drink, and my stepfather left from the bus during a rest break, and the only thing he could find or afford was a few pieces of the spiciest chicken that I had ever put in my mouth. And he could only afford two waters, so my sister and I shared one and they shared one. Honestly, it did not matter because I think I could have had ten gallons of water, and it would not have put the fire out in my mouth from that chicken. We laughed about that for years.

When we arrived in Louisiana, we had nowhere to stay so

we ended up staying with my step-grandparents. They lived in a large two-story home that stood next to my step-grandfather's mother's house. That woman was a rare bird and I still, to this day, thank God that He put her in our lives at the time. My step-grandparents did not accept us as their grandchildren. While my parents were able to stay in their home, we had to stay in this little camper that was on their property. There was no food or drink kept in that camper, and we were given one meal a day by them that we had to eat al fresco or in the camper. Two meals a day on the weekend. During the week, we ate breakfast and lunch at school. My stepdads' mother was a mean woman that cursed with every breath and smoked like a chimney. His grandmother, however, was the kindest woman I ever met in my life at that point. We were allowed to go to her house and visit, and she would make us tea cakes and give us whatever we needed. She was a highly creative woman, too, because we liked to travel up to the attic and see her old things. She brought us up there one time and then she could not keep us from trying to go back, so, worried about the potential for us being harmed in such an old house, she told us the tale of "Bloody Bones." He was just a skeleton that lived there, apparently, and was enough to keep us out of there and safe.

My stepbrother came to live with us for a while and my sister, he, and I all stayed in that little camper. The living room was our bedroom as it had a fold-out couch, and my stepbrother slept in the bedroom ten feet away at the end of the hall. There was a small kitchenette in the center and a slim box of a bathroom you could barely fit into. That little camper held a few horrors of its own. My stepbrother would often hit on my sister. He was fifteen and she was twelve. I can't describe the sick relationships and things that happened between all of us children, and wouldn't want to go into detail on anything that did happen then but the shame overwhelmed me quite often; it's just something I thought that I had to do to be accepted by the older kids.

When we left there and moved into another house, my stepbrother moved with us. He and my sister had gotten very strange ideas in their head and decided that they were going to run away with a man that lived in a camper and sold fireworks at a stand about a mile from our house. This man was a true pedophile as both my stepbrother and my sister were still young. This man in his forties was bringing them into his trailer and giving them alcohol and marijuana. I only know this because the one time I accompanied them, I was allowed inside of the trailer only long enough to see drugs and alcohol everywhere and both my stepbrother and sister having drinks put in their hands immediately. The man then told my siblings that I needed to go back home but they could stay. About a week later, they both came to me with this elaborate plan to run away with this man, and they tied me up and told me that when my parents came home to tell them that I knew nothing about them running away, only that they had tied me up and left. The truth is I knew everything about where they were and what their intention was. So, of course, when my parents came home, I told them because I was afraid for their safety even at that early age. They did bring them back home and shortly after that, our stepbrother left to go live with his mother again. My sister, at age twelve, was groomed by one of my stepfather's friends at the time. It was disgusting the way he would inappropriately pay attention to her when he would come to visit my parents. She became so convinced that she loved him, she took me in the middle of the night and ran away to be with him. We walked six miles to this guy's house, and he knew we were coming over there apparently because when we got there, he said, "Glad you got here safe. Come on in."

As soon as we were inside, he told me to stay in the living room and gave me something to drink and the remote to the TV. My sister then followed him into his bedroom where they remained for half an hour or so. I could hear the sounds, and I knew what was going on. I picked up his home phone and called my parents. You can only imagine the chaos that ensued. My sister was intensely angry at me, and that was the first time they dropped her off at the youth shelter. In those times, if you had a troubled child, you could take them to a youth shelter in our hometown and leave them for three days. There, your children were housed, fed, and worked like horses. They were disciplined to try to put them on the right path again. If you did not pick them up within three days, they would become a ward of the state and foster care placement search would begin. If they were not placed in foster care within two months, the parents had the option again to pick them up and take them home. I have my own memories from that place, and I will get to them soon. They did go and pick her up on the third day and bring her home. Shortly after that incident, we moved to a city farther out in the countryside. My sister and I shared a room, and my parents had a room clear across the other side of the trailer. We had quite a few times when we had no electricity and no food in the house, and they would not come home until we were already in bed asleep. They always had money to go drink and buy cigarettes but rarely had money to pay the bills or provide food outside of what they wanted to eat, which they kept in their bedroom, if it was nonperishable, to be sure that we could not access it. We usually had ramen because it was $0.15 a pack and did not cost them very much to feed us three meals that way. As a parent myself, I cannot imagine my child going hungry while I ate whatever I wanted to. And yet that is exactly what they did. They also made room for any pedophile along the way that wanted to take advantage of their children. Our next-door neighbor at the time, we can just call Mr. H— now that is a man who loved children. He just did not love them in a healthy way. We were both molested by him, and he would often give us alcohol to loosen us up, and he would always feed us a satisfying meal after those meetings. Understand this: if you are not involved heavily with your children, someone out there who wishes to harm them will be. They will appear as their knight in shining armor, there to help because they understand them.

It was not long after that that we both ran away again. This time, however, my parents decided to leave us exactly where we were. We did not want to live with them anyway and the group home was a much brighter option, but it was my first time there, and being so young, I was scared. My sister went back to the family that had her when she was young because she told the group home they would want her. She was right; that family loved her very much, but because they had two sons of their own, they did not feel like they could take me as well. We were not the most well-behaved children for obvious reasons, so I do not blame them for not taking on two girls with the history that we had.

After my sister left the group home, I was left by myself with a few other girls that were still in between stops. Every day, we had chores. We were fed well, but we did the cooking and cleaning. One girl horribly bullied me there. It does not matter how many times she was reprimanded for doing so, she would not stop being ruthlessly cruel to me, and she was two years older than me, so she was around the age of thirteen, as I was eleven then. I forget what it was that she did exactly, but she tried to harm me, and they put her in the adult detention center in front of the youth center for four months. When she came back, she was very much a different person. I do not know what happened to her there, but she was sweet when she returned. My guess is some of the people in there must have made her feel like she made me feel and that made me sad for her. We became close friends until I left a few weeks later to go into my first foster home after the group home. I still wonder what happened to her, and I pray that God has a hand in her life and that she knows Him because she has been through so much trauma as well.

# CHAPTER FOUR

The second foster family I spent time with were not nice people. They were a married couple with no children of theirs, but quite a few foster children had seen those walls.

I was enrolled in middle school at their home at the age of twelve, and I stayed at their home for three months before I was removed. They were not using my monthly clothing allowance to buy me clothing and, in fact, I was not even aware there was a monthly clothing allowance. I was borrowing clothes from the other girl who was in the home at the time who was five sizes bigger than me. I called my probation officer they assigned me (everyone was assigned a probation officer after being in a group home, no matter the reason you were there). I was just going to tell him that I needed some clothes because I did not know how to get any, and he was incredibly angry. Not with me but the people with whom I was staying. I asked him to please not say anything because I did not want to get in trouble as they were already rude to us constantly, and I remember him telling me that was unacceptable, and he would be there in a few minutes. I will never forget him because he stood up for me.

I cannot tell you how rare it was to have someone stand up for me back then. He took me and paid for me to have clothes out of his own pocket. When he brought me home, he told them he was working on getting both me and the other girl out of there from that very moment and until that day they had better be absolutely sugar and spice to us because everything that happened and happens from that point on would be going in a report. He told them that if they did not want to face charges of child neglect, they would happily comply with what he told them. I pray for him too.

God placed people in my life when I felt like no one would ever care about me—outside of my brother, who obviously did but was no longer around at this stage in my life. Honestly, he had not been there to protect me most of my life at that point, so I knew that the best way to protect myself was to shrink down and be quiet. People cannot get mad at something they can't see.

I was placed in a new foster home with a woman who worked in a salon and her girlfriend. The girl that I was in the previous foster home with went as well. I was so thankful that she was there because as soon as we got there, my monthly started, and I was scared to death because I didn't know what to do. She helped me figure it all out and as quickly as that happened, she was put into a different home, and I was left there by myself. When I left my previous school, I left behind a boy that I liked very much, and I asked them if I could still talk to him on the phone. They were absolutely against it, and I do not know why other than I was young and did not really need a boyfriend at the time. The girl there with me was older, and she stood up for me, telling them that I needed to have some connection with the few people that were still in my life. They did not like that, so they sent her to another home and kept me there with them.

I spent the summer with them before I ran away. I was found shortly after I ran away but obviously, they did not want me to return there and that was okay with me. I was placed back in the group home for around three weeks and then I was told I would be going to live with a pastor and his wife. At that time, that was the last thing I wanted to hear...

When I arrived at their home, I was greeted with this short, dark-haired woman playing a guitar. I rolled my eyes hard enough to see the back of my brain as we pulled into the driveway. They took me to church regularly. The girl cousin, who perpetrated her own crimes against me, was a youth leader, so I had no desire to be around people who went to church anymore. To me, God was nothing more than someone that people talked about, and I didn't understand what the big deal was.

When I got out of the car, she greeted me by singing the song, "What a Mighty God We Serve."

I rolled my eyes again but smiled sweetly because I wanted them to let me stay there. I was tired of moving around. I was ushered into the house by this short little smiling woman who seemed absolutely overjoyed that I was there. I knew it had to be fake because she didn't know me, and I didn't know her.

That sweet woman was the furthest thing from fake in my life.

That night was the beginning of the revival at their church, and she took me to the local store to grab something to wear as I really had nothing more than a few comfortable clothes in a trash bag. I picked out the prettiest pink dress that, to me, looked like what a sophisticated woman would wear. I can still see it in my mind. I had never seen anything so pretty. After picking out what I needed, she took me back to the house and promptly began rolling my hair in tight little curlers. I had told her I wanted my hair curled for church that evening and she took it to the next level by giving me a home perm. Thank You, Jesus, that I was young and social media did not exist!

I loved it at the time to be honest. Until I met some of the other kids from church. Anyway, I had gone to church that evening very unsure of anything other than I thought I looked pretty for the first time ever. I sat on the pew next to them, listened to the praise and worship songs, and just looked around. After the charge, we went home, and I was able to lay down in a bed that did not feel like a rock for the first time in a while. The thing I hated was the large tape player by my bed that she came in and turned on. It was Scripture read from the Bible and I thought, *Oh, I will never be able to get to sleep.* Oddly enough, I fell asleep within a few minutes.

The next morning, I was greeted with a smile and a song before my eyes even opened. It was the same song that I had heard before loudly being played on the guitar and sung *loud-ly*!

My face must have had a crazy expression on it because she looked at me and just started laughing. She gave me a big hug and said, "Come eat breakfast, darling!"

Who was this woman? So bubbly and happy all the time, when I had no idea about happiness in general. I was irritated by her constant happiness when I was in the moment those first few weeks. But she had the true joy inside of her that I wanted inside of me, and I was determined to figure her out. At thirteen years old, I was certain that I had it all figured out—or at least had figured out what I had to do to protect myself.

That night we went back to the revival as it was a week-long event. That was also the night my life changed in a way I did not know was possible. Well, not my whole life at that point but my heart. I always had a tender heart towards people, even through everything, but that night, as I invited Jesus to live in my heart, at first it was simply because I thought it was what they wanted me to do. However, when I spoke that prayer, a peace and chills like I had never felt, came over me, and I began crying harder than I ever had. Suddenly, I did not recognize the language that was coming from my mouth. A warmth flowed through my entire body, and I spoke in this foreign-to-me language for a solid minute. It seemed like longer to me, but when I stopped and looked over, this cute little woman sitting next to me hugged me tightly. She said that God had used me to speak a word to the people there that night. I remember I could hear the pastor on stage speaking in the background as the words flowed from my mouth. And he translated what God was saying. I honestly do not remember what she told me in that moment; I just remember the power that I felt inside of me and the peace that really does surpass all understanding.

They owned a print shop in the downtown area and through that summer, I would work with them stapling booklets or anything that they really needed help with. Every Sunday after church, we would go to a rehabilitation hospital and minister to the people that were there, unable to make it to church. When the fall came, they made a deal with the local Christian academy that they would do all the printing for them that year for free in place of my tuition; it was an expensive school, but they made the sacrifice so that I could be surrounded at school by God and people who loved Him as well. I did not have a pleasant experience at that school. I did have fun running track and being on dance line, but the material was hard because no one ever helped me in schooling and it was more advanced than the public schools around there, and honestly the kids were not nice; at least not any nicer than those in public school. I was thankful for the opportunity in every way, and I did the best I could in my studies, but I still barely passed the ninth grade. At fourteen years old, I really struggled with everything around me, and just because I had accepted Jesus into my heart, it did not mean that things changed immediately for my thought processes or the way I felt inside. I did feel different in a small way, like I was safe in the moment. I cannot sit here and tell you that the instant you accept Christ into your heart everything will be like a fairy tale and the birds will sing and everything will change, and you never have to suffer or feel negativity again. That is just not true. When you accept Christ, God begins a magnificent work inside of you. That work that He wants to do requires a refining of your heart and your mind. Growth, as I have said, is extremely uncomfortable. Healing trauma that no one ever apologized for is a tricky thing to do, but it is not impossible because nothing is, with God. The thing about God is He will never impose His will on you. You can invite Him into your life, and He still will not make you do anything that you do not want to do.

This is why we must know the history of the God we serve and get an understanding of why He does not want us to do certain things in life. Every bit of the reasons that you should not partake in some things from this world, all correlate to your abundant life, or lack of, in this life. It took me a long time to realize that I was bringing on my own issues, and even though there were outside forces involved, I played a huge role by seeking love where there was none, from people who never intended to be there for me.

The next summer, they decided to move away and pastor a church in another state. They could not take me with them because of regulations in place concerning foster care. Thankfully, I had met a good friend in the neighborhood that became my best friend, and her mother and father gladly took me in when they had to move.

I was moving to yet another home, but this time, I was taking away a few more clothes and personal items and the beginning of a very personal relationship with Christ. It may not have been the end of my trying times, not by a long shot, but it was the first stage of changing my view.

# CHAPTER FIVE

Living with my friend's family was a new experience and the first time I had ever seen what it would be like if my own mother and father were healthy people. Her parents and brother were nice people and very down-to-earth. We would go on evening walks as a family, and they always seemed like they were there to talk to. One time in my high school, while I was living with them, a teacher was extremely, horribly rude to me in front of the whole class. Honestly, I am sure he was tired of my smart mouth because at the time I hated the world. No one ever taught me what it was like to act and react in a healthy manner. Even so, the things he said were out of line, and when my friend's mother found out, she very calmly but firmly told him she would be reporting everything he said to the principal and the school board. That was one of the only times an adult had ever come to my defense. I felt conflicted because I wanted to stay with them, but I also wanted to see my mother again. I did not know at the time, but they had to go through the state and a fostering program which they were doing months before I moved in with them, because their daughter had told them that I needed to be in a safe place. Yes, the pastor and his wife were great, but I also complained to my friend a lot because they were extremely strict, and I had never experienced that before. Some things that they did would now be considered abuse, I think, but there was never any physical abuse, and I know that they only had the best intentions. While I was there, they had managed to track down my mother, whom I had not seen since elementary school. Of course, I wanted to meet my mother, so when they told me that they had found her, I immediately asked to see her. They offered to take me the next night as they were trying to contact her to okay this but could not. When we arrived at my mother's trailer, it was after dark but still only around 7:30 p.m. I walked up and knocked on the door with them standing supportively behind me. I cannot even describe how nervous and expectant I was. I wanted my mother to open the door and grab me in her arms and hug me tightly like she had missed me the entire time. What I got was something entirely different. My mother answered the door, and she appeared to have been asleep. The first thing she said to me was, "What the f— are you doing here?" I know, warm fuzzy feeling, right? I told her I just wanted to see her because I had not seen her in years. I guess because they were standing behind me and she did not want to appear to be an awful mother, she invited us in. We visited for thirty awkward minutes, after which I begged her to let me come live with her. She was my mother. I wanted to be near her.

I was met with all the excuses you can imagine why that could not happen, and I left there devastated.

My sister, whom I had not seen since living with my mother, contacted this family when she found out where I was and wanted me to live with her and her new husband. She was seventeen, and he was abusive. Unfortunately, I did not become aware of this dynamic until I went to live with them because obviously, I wanted to see and be with family. That desire never goes away no matter how badly you are treated, until you become healthy.

In the first couple of months of living with my sister, they took me to a bar they frequented. I remember the name but again I am not mentioning names of places because of the people that are in this story. They are still alive, and it is not my goal to oust them in any way. We entered this bar. I was nervous because I was only fifteen and certain that my secret was going to be discovered, and I would be told to leave. The owner and bartender looked at me, and my sister told the story that I was from out of town and all my luggage was lost on the plane including my ID. She told her I was eighteen and that was that. I did not look anywhere near eighteen at fifteen years old, but I don't think it mattered one way or another to the owner if she made money. We began drinking and this was my first time drinking so it only took a couple of drinks before I was inebriated. We laughed and had some fun, told some jokes, and then left around midnight or 1:00 a.m. All of us had been drinking and her husband had been drinking the most heavily, yet he was driving us. As soon as we got to the house, they were in an argument about something, and he backhanded her in the front yard. I jumped on his back and started hitting him in the head and told him if he ever touched my sister again, I would kill him. He threw me off and hit my back hard on the ground, knocking my breath out of me for a moment. He turned around to hit me, and my sister jumped on his back. I did not even realize how dysfunctional this was because this is all I had ever really known other than a couple of people that I had managed to get a peek inside of their lives. I was there for three months, and it was a lot of drinking and partying and arguing and violence. Still, I just wanted to be with my sister.

When she tried to enroll me in the high school close to her, she figured out that she did not have the authority to do so because I had just left to live with her without letting anyone know other than the family I was with. When she called my mother to ask her to sign the enrollment forms, suddenly my mother would not have it and brought me to live with her.

My high school years were fraught with abuse verbally and physically at the hands of my mother. She was an alcoholic and would wake up in the morning and fill her 44 oz cup mostly with vodka and a splash of orange juice. She was what was called a functional alcoholic because she was able to go to work and maintain her job as a server while drinking all day. She did eventually lose that job when she got a little too drunk at work and it became apparent what she had been doing. If I were sick, it did not matter, as she would still treat me like I was a plague in her existence and my illness was just another problem she had to deal with. I can remember her telling me "I love you" three times in my entire life. There are so many memories of her making fun of me and calling me horrible names.

She is still alive, though she does have heart trouble, and we do not talk. I did try to have a relationship with my mother as an adult, but when it seemed like all she wanted was money and not to be there for me, I decided to cut her off from my life.

When my daughter was eighteen months old, they diagnosed me with CIN1, which is not yet cancer but something they watch for six months to see if it remains active and grows. I told my mother I feared not knowing for that long. She sympathized for a moment and then made a social media post, telling everyone her daughter had cancer. I even commented on the post that it is not cancer, just active cells. Within a few months, her and my sister got together and decided to shut me out, then saying I lied about having cancer! It was amazing to me how they twisted everything to that point. My mother was famous for shutting out her other children for one that was serving her best. It is hard, but when you find a toxic pattern that exists within a family member and you realize that that family member only causes you to be in turmoil, sometimes you must cut them out of your life. It is easier to do with friends or acquaintances but anyone who demands that you give, and they only take, should not have access to you.

As you read earlier in this book, my mother suffered traumas at the hands of my father, my brothers' father before that, and her father before that. She did finally find an amazing man in my stepdad, and he always tried to keep her from being too horrible to us, though most of the time that just resulted in an argument between them. My stepfather was a calm man. He was not easily perturbed by much, a stark contrast to my mother. When he passed, I had already cut my mother from my life and found out through my brother. I tried to reach out and was told by my mother, through my sister in text messages, that I was never his daughter. While that was painful, I understood why. She was bitter that I stopped playing into her narcissistic view of herself.

# CHAPTER SIX

My mother emancipated me at the age of sixteen years old. I was in high school and dating a boy, and since I had no real example of a healthy relationship, I let him coerce me one night into being intimate. I remember we had drunk quite a bit at a party with a few others behind the high school. I remember being dizzy, and he was pressuring me, telling me that he loved me, and he would never leave me. I had no idea that it was all lies and even though I felt extremely uncomfortable because of the past abuse I had suffered, we still went forth. It was really the only way that I knew a man that loved me to that point, because of the abuses of the past. Even though I had said emphatically that I was not ready, I was made to feel in that moment like I was an outcast if I did not. Call it coercion if it makes you feel better, but if a girl says no, it should be no, otherwise it is date rape. I still want to distance myself from that terminology, but I know the feeling that I had when all of it was taking place. I ended up pregnant from that encounter and when I had to tell my mother, she did what she always did and completely went off on me. I told her I would get an abortion, thinking that would appease her so she did not have to deal with a young, pregnant daughter, but she screamed at me louder and said that would never happen. She had lost a baby boy that was to be the only child between her and my stepfather. I remember when she was pregnant; she was incredibly happy, even though we were living in some no-tell motel with a kitchenette and could hardly afford anything. I wanted that happiness for her, but she was never happy for longer than a few moments. She always made us feel like a huge burden and even said to my sister, "The sight of you makes my stomach turn." I stayed with her until one month after my child was born. A friend of mine in high school whom I was close to at the time knew of my situation and knew how my mother treated me. My mother never helped after the birth, even though they immediately put me on antidepressants that made me fall asleep easily, and I needed someone to help. I knew nothing about being a mother and had no support around me. My friend spoke to her parents, and they converted the formal dining room into a bedroom with a crib and a bed. They enrolled me in GED classes, though it would still be several years before I took the test to get my GED. I could not have done that without her mother watching my child so I could go to finish my high school education. They taught me how to drive and I am certain the truck gears had to be replaced because it was hard learning to drive on a stick shift! That led later to a short career as a truck driver. It was during this time that my mother emancipated me completely and legally because she did not want to be responsible for my "mess ups," as she called them. Within another four months, she was begging me to come back with her grandchild. I wanted to have a relationship with my mother so much, so even though my friend's parents said it was not a clever idea, I moved back with her and my stepfather.

I was looking for a job in the neighborhood babysitting because I did not have a way to get to work at an establishment. My mother lived in a small town but on the outskirts, and the actual town center was at least seven miles away. She would not watch him while I worked a full-time job either, so I found a job being a nanny to two little boys about four houses over, and I could take him with me. While I was working there, I told the woman of my situation, and her and I would often talk about the abuses I was still suffering at the hands of my mother. It was different this time when I moved back in because it is like she hated me more, but she took over the care of my child more often. I should have known then she had something planned but I was very naïve. The woman offered me to stay there with them and bring my son with me, as long as I kept up my end of taking care of their children. They were nice people, and I decided to tell my mother I would be moving in with them. She had no say of whether I could or not because I was my own legal guardian after the emancipation. She vehemently protested me taking him with me. I wanted my child to be with me, and I was just trying to do what I could at seventeen years old to take care of my baby. She said that she would not allow me to take him, and she would fight me on this. And fight she did. She kicked me out and had a friend of hers from the sheriff's department tell me that I can legally take him, but they would just be coming to pick him back up shortly because child services would be called. Again, so naive, I sobbed and made her promise to take care of him. When she got her way, she hugged me and said, "Don't worry. I will make sure he has the best life." Three weeks later, she was calling me and telling me that I needed to sign papers terminating all my parental rights because it was the best thing for him. She had no legal authority until I signed it. I cried the entire time we were at the attorney's office signing the papers. She had effectively stolen my child from me. It may truly be what was best for him, though, because I was so unstable. I was filled with trauma, rage, and sadness.

I lived with that couple for a little while, taking care of their children and then I met a guy who lived three cities over and "fell in love." I do not know if my tone can be conveyed in writing; however, there is an abundant amount of sarcasm in that! I would find, many times, I was "in love," ignoring all the red flags and the fact that I was a red flag too. That relationship and subsequently, many after, were as toxic as Chernobyl. How could I have a healthy relationship when I did not even understand what one was and was not yet healthy myself. Yes, I had seen some instances of healthy relationships with a couple of the families that I was with in my younger years, but no one ever taught me how to process the traumas I had been through so I could become healthy. During that relationship was when I attempted to leave this earth. I was ready to be finished with everything on this earth. My son was taken from me, and I missed him intensely. I was alone one day while my boyfriend was out doing his own thing as always, and I decided to try and overdose on muscle relaxers. I figured the heart was a muscle, so it would relax to the point of stopping if I took enough of them. I did speak to a friend of mine on the phone prior to taking them and said to her, "If you come by later and I don't answer the door, just come in." She happened to decide to come over two hours early and called the paramedics. If it were not for her, I would not still be on this earth, and that was God intervening in the enemy's plan to take my life and, with it, all the people that will have and will come to know God because of my story. God did not cause these things to happen to me. Poor choices by the people that were supposed to be taking care of me and poor choices by me led to the situations I found myself in. I know there were people praying for me even at this time because the preacher and his wife that I lived with told me later in life that they never stopped praying for me. I do believe that God can intervene in your plan if He has planted that seed inside of you. I had accepted Christ fully at fourteen, I just was not living for Him yet. Being in the hospital was bad because the doctors there had no empathy whatsoever for a young girl of eighteen that had just tried to end her own life. When I returned home to my boyfriend, he said that he was so scared, and he never wanted me to leave. Two weeks later, we split because he found someone else. It played at my mother's heart as well because I moved back into her house for around a few weeks, until I found my first roommate situation in some apartments as far as I could get from my mother.

# CHAPTER SEVEN

The next several years, I went through a period where I was fully immersed in the world. I was working in a nightclub and partying all hours of the night after we left. I was determined to drown out all the memories of my life up to that point. I had numerous relationships and all of them fell apart within months. One of those was a friendship when I was twenty-two years old, and we had never dated; we stayed up all night drinking coffee and laughing. We ended up sleeping together. He was eighteen years older than me, and not having the father figure I needed growing up is what led to me dating a series of men that were much older. It is true that a father shapes his daughter's view on relationships. Again, I ended up pregnant. I told this man that I was pregnant, and he informed me that he was sterile, and he and his ex-wife could never have children which is why they divorced. He gave me $500 to get an abortion, but this time I was determined that no one was going to take my child from me. I got a job at a daycare and worked to pay for my own place so my son would have a stable place to be when he came into this world. Between being on benefits and the money I was making, I was able to afford to buy a small car outright and I was happy to be caring for myself. I ended up in a relationship while I was pregnant, that lasted until my son was four months old. I contacted my son's real father and told him that if he wanted a paternity test, he should set it up and that he does have a son, and he should get to know him. He did the paternity test and then he became this overjoyed version of himself. He was so happy to have a child, a son. Then he decided, when I declined his offer of marriage, that he would fight me for him in court because he could offer him a better life; even though I offered him a comfortable life. My son was cared for completely without his help, but he was bitter that I had not told him about him right after the birth, as he assumed I had an abortion. What right did he have to request that of me when he told me that it couldn't be his and gave me the money to end it? Anyway, coparenting with him was a nightmare, and he did have custody for a little while because his attorney met me in the hallway on the day of our court date and had me sign papers saying that he had full custody, and I had reasonable visitation. He convinced me, obviously still very naïve, that I would never get joint custody right now but could get it back if I signed voluntarily and became more financially stable. I found out a few months later, the judge that had presided over the case was extremely angry that his attorney had lied to me on this and not allowed me to be in court to plead my case with him. Again, another son was ripped from me. Yes, I was allowed to see him regularly, but it was not the same because I had been the one to care for him completely from the moment I was pregnant with him. When his father tried to get me to be in a relationship with him when he first found out about him for the second time, I was not interested because he had been so unsupportive and outright mean to me. After that, he made it clear that he would do everything he could to get back at me including poisoning my son's view of me during the time that he lived with him from two years old to four years old. My son lived with me and my ex-husband from the time he was four until he was nine, when our relationship ended. There had come a point after a bad business deal with the purchase of my son's father's business by another man, that his father went bankrupt. The deal had produced a large amount of money at the onset, but bad investments drained him a couple of years later. I talked him out of taking his life for five hours when my son was three and a half years old and told him I would gladly bring my son to live with me and he could still see him as often as possible. I even picked him up every week after he sold his house and moved to a hotel and brought him to our home to visit his son. And yet, in the years that he had my son from age nine and a half to eighteen, he spoke so horribly about me and even to this day, my son refuses to have me as part of his life. I will not pretend that he is the only reason that my son has come to this because before my healing, I was an extremely reactive parent. I did not hit my child, but I still yelled and screamed at my child. When you are trying to break the cycle of abuse by being better to your children, if your parents were abusive, it takes time and hard work. Because I was always yelled and screamed at, I yelled and screamed for many years, and honestly there are times when I still must work on this because we can slip back into the flesh if we do not make the daily choice to be our new selves. Being a Christian does not mean you are perfect; it means that you are constantly battling the person that you used to be, the person that the world would have you be. It means that you are choosing daily not to revert to those behaviors that were part of your life before you accepted Christ. Christ is love and it takes a lot to operate in love when you were never shown love. I believe, one day, that relationship will be restored because I know how big our God is.

# CHAPTER EIGHT

I was unhealed when I met my ex-husband. I had no business entering marriage in the mental and emotional state that I found myself in those days. I was still angry at the world and looking to be loved so much that I was willing to put up with anything. My ex-husband was very wealthy. He had a geology firm with a geologist partner, and he was a geophysicist. He was eighteen years my senior. He was freshly out of his first marriage that lasted eighteen years and living in an apartment with his eldest daughter. I absolutely adored him. In the beginning of our marriage, I was adjusting to his four children and had my son and his eldest daughter living full time with us. The others would visit on the weekend and his middle daughter joined living with us in the first six months. She was the toughest one and would purposely sabotage things between him and me.

I was working full time as an executive administrator, and my son was enrolled in a private school to allow him to receive more private instruction so that the next year he could gain acceptance into the magnet program. I was also still very volatile and explosive over every little thing. The children, naturally, did not like me in the beginning, other than the eldest daughter. I cannot tell you what it feels like to be shunned in your own home continually but for me it was nothing new. Unfortunately, I had experienced that all my life growing up wherever I was, so I could endure it, but it did not feel good. I would often explode in yelling and screaming fits when I was angry. I would get up and go to church on Sunday mornings with my husband and my new little family and then by the evening I would end the evening yelling and screaming at him about something. I was in church, but I was not allowing God to operate in me. My ex-husband is the one that said, "You need therapy." He was right. I was angry about him calling me out on it, but he was right. I began seeing a counselor at the behavioral health center where I worked for several years as a mental health tech. Talk about ironic, right? I discovered a lot about the trauma I was holding onto in therapy and discovered the best way to deal with them in that moment. You must feel the pain and process it to heal. I could not keep numbing myself and expect to heal. I did not completely heal in the two years that I attended counseling, but it started me on the right path. When you have trauma like I had, or worse, it can be a lifelong journey. Healing is not linear, so some days can feel like you've taken two steps back on your journey or you can sit in one place for a while. God can take away the shame and help you lessen the pain of your experiences. I spoke about free will and because of free will so many have suffered. But if you have suffered, you can choose to become bitter and go after everything in this world or you can be better and feel a sense of peace you have never felt.

Shortly after healing from those past traumas, I faced a

whole new one. I suspected infidelity in my marriage for quite some time but could gather no concrete proof. I was sitting on our patio looking down at the park area that was at the base of a sloped hill on which our home was situated. I was praying and asking God that if there was infidelity in my marriage, and I should leave, I needed a burning bush sign. The gut feeling, that I now know is a sign from God, was not enough in the moment. In an instant, in the blink of an eye, hundreds of thousands of dragonflies descended and landed all over the park, our vehicles, our home, and me. It was a beautiful, remarkable sight. They flew all around me for around a minute or two. I was so immersed in the experience of being heard by God, and I cannot truly remember how long they remained. I began sobbing and thanking God that He answered in such a way. It left no room for doubt. Then they disappeared. It is not like they flew off in the manner that they had descended; they just weren't there anymore. I made my decision then to divorce and promptly let him know that's what I wanted. I told him I couldn't prove that he was being unfaithful, but I suspected it, and he would not admit it, so I didn't feel I had trust left in me with him. I told him God had clearly shown me that there was infidelity going on and that I would not stay with someone who denied it even in the face of God. I had signed a prenuptial agreement with him and knew that I would be walking away with only what I had. That was okay with me because I was not after the money he had. I was after a genuine and loving marriage which we did not have. I had confirmation from God. Admittedly, I was questioning my decision within moments after moving day, but I still knew God sent the sign to guide my path. People think marriage is something you should never leave. It is what I thought and why I was so torn as to cry out to Him for a definitive answer. I do take my vows before God seriously. However, most will not understand, when they are facing divorce, that they may have been unequally yoked from the beginning. God does not want you to be unequally yoked because it will end in the dissolution of a marriage eventually and cause many anxieties whilst involved. A friend and I were out a couple of months after the divorce and my ex-husband's secretary was in the same establishment that evening. She approached me and said she was sorry to hear of my divorce. I said thank you and asked her to sit down. She began crying and telling me that she was having an affair with my husband. It had been going on for two years of our four-year marriage.

Still to this day, when I am facing anything, God will confirm with dragonflies. Not in the massive swarm that was present that day, but one or two or more if it is something big. There really is freedom in dragonflies for me. I feel such a sense of peace that does surpass all my understanding.

# CHAPTER NINE

When I think about the traumas that I suffered in the past, I do not think of them in the same way I did before. Instead of looking at what was done to me, I decided to think of what it has done for me. The drive to completely change things and the failure to change them on my own, brought me into God's purpose for my life. I would not be the same person I am today without having experienced those things. I thank God every day for the grace to have overcome the shame of the past and the grace He gives me every day of my life. I am still not perfect, and I won't be until I reach heaven. I do not want to be perfect. I want those out there that are broken by things that have been done to them or the wrong choices they have made, to be healed and see the healing that comes from a real relationship with Christ. I searched for fulfillment in this world for most of my life. The only thing I found were temporary ways to feel happiness. I never felt true joy and peace until I decided to let Christ take over completely. I always felt a void at the end of the day, deep inside my soul, and I could not figure out how to fill it. I was stuck in the cycle of waiting for the next grandiose thing because I knew I would be happy when that happened. The only problem was, when the next important thing came, it did not bring the joy I expected, and when that moment of happiness faded, I was still not happy. When you live that way, there is a constant need for external fulfillment. Trust me when I say the only thing that fills that void is God Himself. I will not lie to you and tell you that it happens instantly because you must continually seek Him and His plan for your life. When we are fulfilling our purpose, we are as whole as we will be on this earth.

It was not until the last five years of my life that I began to really desire to grow closer to God and see where it led. It has led to Him opening doors I never thought possible for me to help others in a way that I never dreamed. When I look back at the path He took me on to bring me to my current state of being, I can see how it all worked together for my good. At the time I was going through all these things, I did not believe there was any way I would ever be where I am at this moment. The person I am now, compared to the person I was even five years ago, is the epitome of a new creature. I look back often at the memories of that little girl that I was, and I am baffled by what God has done to create this new person. I became the person that I needed when I was younger. I became the chain breaker in our family so that those generational curses that were heaped upon me and my siblings would not be put on my children. This did not magically happen. I had to make a choice every day to get up and seek Him on how to be this version of myself. Every day, even when I do not feel like a new being, I make the choice to live in His promises. People will say they do not believe in God because of the things that happen in this world. If you decide to keep your eyes on this world that is all you will ever see. Our freedom of choice is ingrained into the deepest part of us because He created us that way. It breaks my heart that there are so many that have decided to be ruthlessly evil in this world, but God is not the cause of that, outside of giving them free will. When you are tired of chasing the world and coming up empty-handed, ask God to show you who He is. I will put it like this: if I am wrong, the only thing I did was make this world a better place. I loved harder, spoke softer, and was a comfort to as many people in this world as I could be. If there is no eternity, as a lot believe, then at least my time here was well spent. However, if I am right, as I believe, my eternal peace is guaranteed when I leave this earth. I will have no more painful memories of the past, and I will be surrounded by such a love that nothing here compares with. I do not say this lightly: if you do not know Christ today, give Him the chance to change your life. I do not know what hell will be like, but I do know an eternal separation from God is the absence of light and love and warmth. Could you imagine being in a place where there is no light? You have seen what this world looks like currently, so you have experienced at least some of what it looks like to suffer to no end. Do you want to take the chance of that being your *eternity*? I encourage you to say this prayer aloud if you are ready to see the change happen in your life.

*Dear Lord Jesus, I know that I am a sinner, and I ask for Your forgiveness. You died for my sins and rose from the dead. I turn from my sins and invite You to come into my heart and life. I want to trust and follow You as my Lord and Savior.*

My prayer for you is that you have said this prayer, and

you are willing to seek Him. Blessings to you all. If you need further guidance, you may email me @ Radixcausatherapy@ gmail.com